The #1 Guide To:

Budgeting: Personal Finance

Budgeting, Personal Finance, And Gaining Financial Freedom In An Easy To Follow System That Will Change Your World!

James Harper

STOP!!! Before you read any further....Would you like to know the Secrets of Transforming your life, overcome insecurities, develop leadership skills, and undeniable confidence in your personal, professional, and relationship life?

If your answer is yes, then you are not alone. Thousands of people are looking for the secret to have unstoppable confidence and self-driven power in all areas of their lives.

If you have been searching for these answers without much luck, you're in the right place!

Not only will you gain incredible insight in this book, but because I want to make sure to give you as much value as possible, right now for a limited time you can get full **100% FREE access to a VIP bonus EBook** entitled **LIMITLESS ENERGY!**

<u>**Just Go Here For Free Instant Access:**</u>

www.PotentialRise.com

Legal Notice

Disclaimer Notice

information contained herein on the new conditions whenever they see applicable.

Table Of Contents

Introduction

I want to thank you and congratulate you for purchasing the book, *"#1 Budgeting Personal Finance Plan - A Money Makeover Budgeting Plan that will literally Change Your World!"*

In some way, we're all living within a budget. Our lives are a circular progression of earning and spending, and earning and spending again. Since this cycle is inevitable if we are to survive, the values we hold about money are put to the test when we know that we're running out of money, when we're considering debt, and when we're anticipating stress.

Since we're all operating on a certain budget limited by our income, we have our own ways of managing our money such that most of us run out of it, some of us live paycheck to paycheck, and a few manage to set aside something for the future. The difference between these three groups of people involves sound budget, or simply put: living within one's means.

Nowadays, more people are entertaining the idea of having a budget. This is probably the result of the recent economic downturn the world has experienced. Regardless, budgeting is the operative word if you want to enjoy the benefits of your earnings. Don't be like a one-day-millionaire. This book will hopefully teach you how to do it.

This book contains proven steps and strategies on how to change your personal financial present and future through this amazing budgeting plan!

Thanks again for purchasing this book, I hope you enjoy it!

Chapter 1: Why Budget?

Financial control

Money should never control you; it should be the other way around. When money controls you, you tend to live a one-day-millionaire-s life characterized by extravagance and orientation to the present. Because money tells you that you earn it to spend it, you commonly find yourself stressed, wondering where your money went to, and in debt.

On the contrary, if you control your money, you won't be living the kind of life reminiscent of a millionaire, but you save yourself from stress, worry, and debt. Financial control means that before you even touch your money, you know where it's supposed to go, how you're supposed to spend it, and when you'll spend it. This is where budget comes in.

Financial tracker

Count how many times you've thought about not knowing where your money went. Count the number of times when you got shocked that your money's almost gone. Count the number of times when that money supposedly for your savings account was used anyway. During those times, you probably have felt as though you still have enough in your account.

When it comes to money, it is easy to commit calculation errors, and sometimes, these errors can be fatal. If you miss a payment, you'll get hit with fees; and when that happens, you'll find it difficult to recover. Budgeting helps you track how you spend your money, and as it gets depleted, you'll know how to strategize your spending.

Financial goals

Have you ever been overwhelmed with the desire to possess something the first time you laid eyes on it? Have you ever been tempted to get it because you had the money? If not, how soon were you able to get it? And how did you eventually get it? These questions point to the simple goal-setting methods we employ helps us stabilize our budget.

In contrast to what most people believe, we are establishing a goal when create a budget. And because the amount of money we wish to spend on something becomes the goal, we make compromises. For example, we might opt to forego buying a new Smartphone so we can finally take home an HD television.

Financial striving

Budget not only tells us how much money we have. It also tells us how much money we need to raise. In ordinary conversations, we call this the act of "making ends meet." What if we don't have enough to make those ends meet? This is where the power of budgeting benefits us.

Just like compromising, budgeting tells us whether or not we need to work more, or whether or not we need to look for other sources of income. Because we know that budgeting is goal-setting in itself, we can see how our long-term financial plans are coming along. We can also see how we can make adjustments to our short-term goals to make our money just enough to make such ends meet.

Financial health

Budget reveals three things: how much money we have, how much money we need, and how much money we can still save. By looking at these aspects, we're able to analyze how we our finances are. We also come to know how good we are at making money, at spending money, and at saving money. Financial health doesn't mean financial freedom. In fact, financial freedom is a myth because even billionaires benefit more if they live on a budget. Financial health then refers to how we generally appraise our financial condition hence, it is highly subjective. Some of us might say that our budget adequately reflects our financial wellness while other may say that they need to do more in order for their budget to be effective.

Chapter 2: Myths About Budgeting

Budgeting is deprivation disguised as a need

The notion of deprivation here needs to be clarified: first, if you want to have something but you can't get it because you're penniless, then you're depriving yourself. If you have a budget that accommodates extra savings on your wants, you'll be able to get what you want. So budgeting is not a self-imposed deprivation.

Budgeting is not for the affluent

Wrong! As your income increases, your expenses also increase. Besides, you're liable to pay more taxes, so you really need a budget to avoid any legal liabilities. In addition, if you are affluent, you are prone to seek advice about wealth management. Why? It's because you want to preserve it. And other than that, the most practical way for you to keep your treasures is by keeping a personalized budget.

Budgeting is only for the shopaholics

You might not spend that much, but how concentrated is your income? Studies show that budgeting is not really beneficial for people who shop individual items. This is because single-item shoppers confine themselves to the price ceiling they set making them prone to miss cheaper options. However, those who do aggregate shopping (like groceries) enjoy more savings because they have a ceiling for what they spend.

Budgeting requires time

When you ruined your financial life, it requires time too, isn't it? In fact, repairing damaged finances will take more energy and time for you because you might be devoting years to things fixed. In the contrary, if you devote at least an hour of your time to create a budget once a month, twice a month, or every payday, you'll keep yourself updated about your finances. So time is not really an excuse.

Budgeting requires mathematics

Of course, it does. But by doing basic arithmetic using a calculator or software, your life is made easier. You won't deal with radicals, exponents, or the Pythagorean Theorem (what?) when you budget. So do yourself a favor by allowing yourself to exercise your mathematical and logical side through budgeting.

Learning Budgeting Secrets – Every Step of the Way

Are there really secrets to personal budgeting? If so, how come everyone doesn't seem keen towards knowing what it is? Well, these secrets are actually called best practices. In the succeeding chapters, we'll go through the different practices involved in personal budget management. We'll go through each of these practices by following the flow involved in creating a budget. Now, before we start, let's clarify two terms first.

Expenditures list – this is the raw list you make in order to determine a budget. You know that budgeting basically means allotting money to cover for expenditures. In effect, an expenditure list outlines the items that you will budget your money for.

Budget – in this chapter, budget refers to the result of creating an expenditures list and budgeting. Hence, budgeting is the act of appropriating money in an expenditures list, and the result of which is the daily, weekly, monthly, or a yearly budget.

Now, the examples we'll work within each chapter are only used to show how to approach budgeting. The figures you'll see there are only meant to represent values in order to help you understand the principle, the method, and the goals of each chapter. As a practical consumer, you can use free tools like Excel to make a budget.

Let's start.

Chapter 3: Personalizing Your Budget

What a good budget should be like

Your budget should be composed of the following: a list of projected expenditures based on your own defined needs, a projected spending pattern that is based on your previous spending history, and money allocations based on predicted expenditures. It shouldn't be based on a generic budget sample or someone else's. To make it personalized, all components should fit your own approach towards financial management.

What you should do

Create a personalized expenditures list first before you create a budget. Your expenditures list heavily lies on your previous spending records. Hence, depending on your preference, you can retrieve documented spending history using various sources for a number of months. To optimize the data and insights you'll get, you might want to consider going through 12 months of your previous transactions.

How

Check your bank account activity online. Take note of the credit and the debits made for each month prior. If you're not into online banking, go through your monthly bank statements. But since budgeting is a recurring activity (yes, it also takes time), you'd want everything to be readily accessible. Consider online banking now to enjoy convenience.

Check your credit card activities online. In the same way as what you've done in your bank account, moving to your credit card history is your next step. You're lucky if you have only one credit card or if you don't own one at all as you remove one of the main cause of stretching your budget later on. But after pulling up your monthly statements or your card activity online, include all of the items under the list you created above.

Assign an expenditure category. Go through the different items on your list now. Then assign a category to each item: is it a want or is it a need? Be careful in categorization errors. The rule of thumb is when an expense is something that you can live without, it's a want.

Note: The resulting should be filed chronologically. If you're using Excel, don't sort your data yet because you'll need to do something in the next step.

What you intend to accomplish

At the end of this step, you should arrive at a representative data of your expenses. Do not try to establish a pattern based on the cost of the items yet. Don't even try to deal with the items you marked as "Wants" as well. There's more you need to do.

Questions to ask

- What initial impressions do you have about your transaction history?
- Are there items that caught your attention right away?

- Are there items that surprised you as something you didn't expect to have spent more on?

If you say yes to all of these questions, then you really need to make a budget because you don't seem aware of how you spend your money. At least that's the factor we're measuring here for now.

Chapter 4: The Importance Of Accuracy In Budgeting

What a good budget should be like

It should reflect accurate income and relative expenses. Meaning, it should tell you how much exactly you're making each month, what expenses you've incurred, and what expenses you might incur in the next month.

What you should do

Track your expenses from paycheck to paycheck.

How

Check your bank account activity online. If you don't have online banking, use your pay slips. Obtain the total number of credits or direct deposits you've received.

Under each payout, obtain the total number of debits you incurred. Do this to both of your bank account and credit card history.

Insert the total obtained per month, per credit, and per debit. If you're using Excel, you need to add rows to mark the total of each month in your expenditures list.

What you intend to accomplish

To obtain the total number of credits and debits on your account based on the frequency of your payroll. So if you say that you live paycheck to paycheck, you might as well create a budget from paycheck to paycheck.

Questions to ask

- Were you surprised at how much money you've earned?
- Are you now thinking, "Where did all of my money go?"
- Do you see a big gap between your income and your expenses?
- Were there times when your expenses went over your income? How often?
- Based on the data you see, how many times did you have to pull money out of your savings account or other accounts to have a cushion?

These questions now transition you to spending frequency. It is undeniable that if we don't spend, we won't lose money. But spending is inevitable, and in some cases, we might not spend often but when we do, it usually involves a large amount of money. We might also spend a lot but it involves small purchases. In the end, it all comes to one thing: your spending frequency affects your ability to manage your money.

Chapter 5: All Expense Paid

What a good budget should be like

It should include all types of expenses: the recurring and non-recurring ones. Non-recurring expenditures include those that you pay for quarterly or annually.

What you should do

Make room for periodic expenses

Review. Review a year's worth of your banking activity in order to identify periodic and/or sudden expenses. Include the items you find in your list of expenses.

Spot. Periodic expenses would include car maintenance, holiday presents, etc. Sudden expenses are something that you have not totally planned at all. This includes hospital bills, car repair, etc.

Reflect. Now, in respect to "wants" or "needs," periodic expenses should ideally fall under "needs." What have you found about these expenses? Were you surprised? We'll deal with what you can do with it as we go along.

What you intend to accomplish

To come up with an exhaustive list of items in order to determine how much money is allotted for unique purchases, and to identify whether or not these unique purchases are a product of need or of want. Finally, these will be your basis in creating a budget that includes periodic expenses in the future.

Questions to ask

- What items made the most of your periodic or surprise expenses?
- How much did you spend on these items?
- Were all of them necessary?

These questions affect the manner at which you decide on the necessity of periodic expenses. For example, if your car took damage multiple times within twelve months, would you rather pay for the same damages in the next year instead of replacing your car? What about medical expenses? Would you opt to pay for your hospitalization each time instead of adding insurance on your budget?

Chapter 6: Categorization Is Key

What a good budget should be like

It should be composed of enough categories that allow you to get a clear picture of where your money goes, but too detailed enough to discourage you from the daunting task of tracking.

What you should do

Every category should have its place.

How

Create categories. From the list of expense types you created, group your purchases according to similarities, purpose, price, purchase frequency, etc. Any form of categorization you think best suits your needs is permitted.

Categorize your expenditures list. Using the "wants" and "needs" of items you created, appropriate all items under specific categories. For example, groceries, which are a need, would fall into the Food Category. As a result, your list would look like the taxonomy of things where all of the items you've paid for will be found.

What you intend to accomplish

To establish a set of categories that represent all of the expenditures incurred within a specific period. This might mean that you'd go as far as pulling up transactions that covers six to twelve months from the present date.

Questions to ask

- How much did you spend per category?
- What category did you spend on the most?
- What items per category can you eliminate?
- Which categories can you impose reduced costs?

In this step, you'll do a little analysis. You need to enter a compromise in order to reduce spending on some items while keeping the others financed. You'll also realize that you might need to add other items in each category. For example, if you got a loan this year, then your monthly payment is something you need to add. In this case, you need to reduce or to give up something to make room for another item.

Chapter 7: Allotment Goes A Long Way

What you should do

Every dollar should have its place

How

Price them. Look at the raw list of items you've chosen. Create a column to accommodate the amount of money spent on each item.

Do not round off. While you think that by rounding off means that you're increasing the amount of money you can potentially save, the result will not give you an accurate overview of how much money is spent on which item.

Appraise your expenditures list. Now, because this step gives you a fair idea of how much money is being left in your account each month, then you should not also ignore including one important item in the list: your personal or family savings. We'll discuss more of this in the next step.

What you intend to accomplish

To make sure that your money is accounted for down to the last centavo, to see how much money is unaccounted for, and to determine the ratio of accounted and unaccounted expenses.

Questions to ask

- How much money is unaccounted for?

- Where do you think did the money go?
- What might have caused you to lose track of such amount?
- What can you do to avoid this from happening in the future?

Chapter 8: Your Savings As An Expense

What a good budget should be like

It should include a section for your savings. In as much you consider your expenditures as the more important items to focus on in your budget, your savings are also important. Don't lose sight of it.

What you should do

Include a section where you can record how much you savings you've been making so far.

How

Savings transfers. Depending on how far back you want to go, you should review your banking transactions and see how much money you've been transferring to your savings account.

Account for everything. If some money is not accounted for, could it be that you dropped them in your piggy bank? If the discrepancy is big enough, then you should review your list and think about what you might have missed or where you might have gone wrong.

Review. This is true in accounting even the do-it-yourself method: the amount of credits should be the same as the amount of debits in a given time period.

What you intend to accomplish

To identify the amount and the frequency of savings you made in a given period.

Questions to ask

- How much savings did you make in the previous months?
- How much savings are you targeting in the next few months?
- By reducing costs, is that target possible?

Most people don't treat savings as an expense. Anything that leaves your account and reduces your income should be considered an expense. Treating savings as non-essential part of the budget causes people to miss their regular deposits. By including it in your budget, you'll always have something for your savings account.

Chapter 9: Everything Is Accounted For

What a good budget should be like:

It should accommodate spending information regardless of the mode of payment used. This is especially that experts and practical people alike recommend that you pay in cash, and that's difficult to track.

What you should do

Create a section in your expenditures list for the mode of payment used.

How

Assign method of payment. In each row of expenditures, make a notation about what mode was used to pay for it.

Be specific. For example, if you say online, did you still use your credit or debit card, or did you use third-party payment processors like PayPal?

What you intend to accomplish

To identify the most frequent methods employed to complete a purchase.

Questions to ask

- How often do you use different modes of payment?
- How much did you spend on each payment method?

These questions are useful if you are to avoid convenient situations that entice you to pay. Remember that spending behavior is triggered by convenience (that explains why online shopping is enjoying huge revenues). By knowing your spending habits, you'll be able to address conditions that make you spend money.

Chapter 10: Insights In Budgeting

What a good budget should be like

It should permit meaningful review of your spending pattern in each category, and should allow you to see where opportunities for cutting costs can be made.

What you should do

Study the expenditures list by identifying your spending pattern on a general level down to the category level.

For example, you might find that you spent more on clothes and utility bills more than food. Under food, you might have spent more on prepared meals rather than home-made meals. These are obvious patterns – something that you can easily identify by looking at costs alone.

After, establishing obvious spending trends, see which items on the list you can give up, and see where you can cut costs.

What you intend to accomplish

Surface-level budgeting. You'll make initial deductions and eliminations based on the items in the expenditure list.

Chapter 11: Goal Setting

What a good budget should be like

It should be a reflection of your financial goals and not a tool for you to track your expenses. Meaning, contrary to what most people believe, what you do when budgeting is thinking about how much money you intend to spend and not how much money you've already spent.

What you should do

Your expenditures list should reflect accurate amount of money spend on each of the items listed under each of the categories.

How

What a good budget should be like: it should allow you to uncover salient spending patterns you weren't aware of. In effect, uncovering such patterns should allow you to appropriate it in your budget, or to cut it off of it for good.

What you should do: go beyond what the numbers tell you.

How:

What other columns in your expenditure list can you make inferences about your spending pattern from? For example, you might discover that you are prone to buy online because you can easily use your credit card or your PayPal account.

Chapter 12: Prepare A Budget

What a good budget should be like

It should motivate you to spend less and to save more.

What you should do

Make your budget easy on the eyes

How

Hide or delete any items you don't want to see on the expenditure list next month or moving forward.

Make the amount of savings big enough to see how it grows each month and moving forward.

In your future expenditure list, include a column where you can place the amount of money you've saved as a result of cutting costs in a specific category.

Prepare a Budget

This is where you create a new budget. You now know your spending history; you already have established trends, determined points where costs can be cut, eliminated items, and so on. Look at the resulting data now. If everything left is something you need, create another spreadsheet that contains the same rows, columns, and items as the previous file. Apply money allocations to each item based on your estimates and on your present income. And moving forward, determine who much money you've spent on each item and under each category. You'll be surprised at the results and how much insights are present by looking at your previous spending history.

Conclusion

Thank you again for purchasing this book on budgeting your personal finances!

I am extremely excited to pass this information along to you, and I am so happy that you now have read and can hopefully implement these strategies going forward.

I hope this book was able to help you understand how to better manage your financial life and helps you to accomplish your goals. Also, if you know of anyone else that could benefit from the information presented here please alert them of this book.

The next step is to get started using this information and to hopefully live a happier, healthier and much more fulfilling life!

Finally, if you enjoyed this book and feel it has added value to your life in any way, please take the time to share your thoughts and post a review on Amazon. It'd be greatly appreciated!

Thank you and good luck!

Preview Of:

How To Be Rich

Discover How To Be Rich Using Money Rules Of The Rich To Make Money, Gain Passive Income, Be Debt Free, And Financially Free In 6 Simple Steps!

Introduction

I want to thank you and congratulate you for purchasing the book, *"Wealth And Power: Discover How The Rich Make Money, Leverage Their Income, And Use Creativity To Gain Financial Freedom!"*.

This book contains proven steps and strategies on how to think and operate your financial affairs like the wealthy.

Have you ever wondered how you can take two people working the same job with the same salary and one seems to always have money while the other seems to always be broke? Or have you ever wondered how a self made millionaire is able to rise out of the lower level of society while another seems to be trapped?

Well, if you have ever contemplated on these things, then you are in the right place! There is a process to wealth creation, some may call it a formula, but it is undoubtedly not the result of luck. If you want to get from A-Z, if you want to get to the top of the mountain, you have to have a roadmap. This is your roadmap.

Sometimes the hardest thing to do is to start! Unfortunately this is also the most important part. If you never start, you will never accomplish anything in life, let alone major ambitions. Please don't delay any longer! Stop putting your future on hold, and begin at once towards the amazing life you were born to live and should already be enjoying! I wish you the best of luck in this endeavor, and hope you will choose this book and its principles to be a part of your exciting accent to the top!

Thanks again for purchasing this book, I hope you enjoy it!

Chapter 1 - Living Within 80% Or Less Of Your Income

The fact that you have an income doesn't mean that you need to spend all those income as you please. Sure you can – but you should not if you want to become rich. Many people believe that they work to live and vice versa, thus making them slaves of the vicious cycle of "working for a living". This need not happen to you, and it certainly would not if you follow the rules on accumulating wealth.

The first thing that you need to remember is that you should live within 80% or less of your income. Yes, you heard it right! You cannot go all out with your pay check if you want to become rich. The next question would be: what would you do with your money?

As a basic rule, you need some part of your income to be able to afford your basic needs, i.e. water, food, clothes, electricity etc. You simply have to, or you will not survive. The good news is that there is no problem with spending on them so long as you put a limit on how much you need to spend. You see, being rich does not mean that you have to deprive yourself of the things you need. After all, you have worked hard for that money and you deserve to have a piece of it.

In spending the money you have earned, make sure that you don't go beyond the allowable limit which is 80%. Remember that the 80% should answer for all the things you need to buy or pay for. This goes to tell that you should not have expenses beyond the 80% limit. If you are earning $1200 per month, make sure that your way of living can be sustained by $960 per month and no more. This should cover your food, water and electric bills, rent (if any), transportation costs, and other expenses. If the $960 is not enough for you to last a month, you need to cut off on expenses that you don't need i.e. movie 3x/month, VIP golf membership dues, etc. In simple words, cut those expenses that would go beyond your limit.

You may ask, "Why do I need to do that when the entire $1200 can cover all that?" The answer is simple – because you want to be rich. How does spending on 80% of your income make you rich? Here's how:

- It puts a limit on spending

Since you have a ceiling on your allowable expenses, it automatically shuts off further spending on your part. The fact that you are only allowed to spend on a certain extent makes you think about *not spending* the rest, hence a spending limit you would not otherwise have.

- It helps you to determine which ones you really need

People often buy things they don't really need, resulting both wasted time and money. But because you are only allowed to spend 80% of your income, you are now forced to determine which ones are among the priority expenses. As such, you will have to dispense with the things you don't really need to prevent wasted resources and focus on the more important things that you need in your life.

- It allows you to have spare money

Spare money is very important in maintaining one's financial stability. Life is very uncertain and more often than not, people won't really have time to prepare for the next expenses to come. Saving 20% of your income helps you to gain some leverage financially, especially in times of need.

- It hones your skill of managing your finances

Some say that people show their ability and discipline best when confronted with boundaries or limitations. Having an

80% spending limit tests your skill in managing your finances, which in turn could hone you to become a better and wiser spender in the long run.

Now that you know what to do with 80% of your income, the next thing that you have to know is what to do with the remaining 20%. What does that 20% represent? How does that 20% make a difference in your way of life?

The remaining 20% of your income represents your savings. It is the spare money that you can count on in times of need, thus giving you some financial security and room for other necessary expenses. It gives you more power financially and more security psychologically because you won't be threatened by life events you never planned or in any way expected. In other words, you would be more economically stable. Such amount can make a huge difference between financial uncertainty and financial stability. Of course you wouldn't want to be on the bad side, would you?

However, do not be too complacent with the fact that you have saved at least 20% of your income in a storage box. The fact is, the way you manage that 20% savings is as important as the way you manage the 80% of your income. If you want to be rich, there is no question that you should manage both WISELY. But exactly how can you do that?

Here are where your savings should go:

- Business Fund

  As you will learn later on, having a business investment is very important in creating wealth. Surely, you would need a capital from which you would build your business. Save a business fund for this goal as early as today so that you will have enough money when the time comes that you are ready to venture into the business world.

- Charity Fund

Set aside being filthy rich – what you need to be is a rich man with a heart. As a person, you need to help people in need whether they are complete strangers or the closest of your friends. As the law of karma always says, helping is an investment in itself. Surely, you want to reap the fruits of your good deeds later on!

- Emergency Fund

    No one knows for sure what will happen next. The future is uncertain and the only way for you to be prepared for what might come is to make sure that your weapons are ready. Have an emergency fund that you can count on anytime and in any event so you won't be caught off guard!

- Car Fund

    A means of transportation is also very essential in building your wealth. In order to be rich, you need to have the ability to move around places as you deal with transactions. This could only be attained by having a reliable means of transport – a car.

    This car fund is not only to be used to purchase a car (if you don't have one yet); it should also be a fund ready to answer for car repairs and improvements.

- Miscellaneous Fund

    Expenses which cannot be classified into a specified group should be covered under miscellaneous fund. This is where you should get the money to finance unexpected, little costs you haven't expected in your budget. This gives you a little leeway for spending on things that you need but failed to account for in your budget.

- Pleasure Fund

  Truth be told, pleasure is a basic human need. Whether it is as grand as having a world cruise or a simple movie per week agenda, your pleasure has to be incorporated in your life.

  All people have their own choices when it comes to what gives them pleasure, some more costly than others. The reason why you need to have a fund to answer for your pleasure expenses is so that you will never have to choose or compromise between necessities and pleasure. You can have both and still be rich! You might think that these funds cannot be covered by the 20% fund alone, and you're correct about that to an extent. But the thing is, these are some of the funds that you can utilize in times of need.

The manner on which you want to distribute the savings is up to you; you may divide the 20% equally or depending on your priorities. If you badly want a car, you may allot more to your car fund that in any other funds. You see, there is no hard and fast rule when it comes to your savings so long as you have these important fund classifications with you. All of these accounts are important for you to attain the financial stability you're aiming for.

To better utilize these funds, you can go to a reliable credit union where you can set up 6 accounts representing each fund. Aside from having them take care of your accounts of you, you can also be sure that you won't be able to spend your money on impulse as when you have the money on hand.

If you don't find (or want) a credit union to handle your savings, you can definitely just use an envelope to separate these funds under one account. Either way, you accomplish your goal of savings utilization by putting up different funds.

Thanks for Previewing My Exciting Book Entitled:

"How To Be Rich: Discover How To Be Rich Using Money Rules Of The Rich To Make Money, Gain Passive Income, Be Debt Free, And Financially Free In 6 Simple Steps!"

To purchase this book, simply go to the Amazon Kindle store and simply search:

"HOW TO BE RICH"

Then just scroll down until you see my book. You will know it is mine because you will see my name "James Harper" underneath the title.

Alternatively, you can visit my author page on Amazon to see this book and other work I have done. Thanks so much, and please don't forget your free bonuses

DON'T LEAVE YET! - CHECK OUT YOUR FREE BONUSES BELOW!

Free Bonus Offer: Get Free Access To The PotentialRise.com VIP Newsletter!

Once you enter your email address you will immediately get free access to this awesome newsletter!

But wait, right now if you join now for free you will also get free access to the "LIMITLESS ENERGY" free EBook!

To claim both your FREE VIP NEWSLETTER MEMBERSHIP and your FREE BONUS EBook on LIMITLESS ENERGY!

Just Go To:

www.PotentialRise.com

www.ingramcontent.com/pod-product-compliance
Lightning Source LLC
Chambersburg PA
CBHW071549170526
45166CB00004B/1602